YOU CAN BE AN ACTOR TOO

Written By: N. C. Lyle
Inspired By: Emma Rayne Lyle
Illustrated By: Burnt Red Hen

Copyright © 2018 by Emma Rayne Lyle and N.C. Lyle
All rights reserved.

Printed in the United States of America. No part of this book may be used or reproduced in any manner whatsoever without written permission except in the case of brief quotations in an article or other noncommercial uses permitted by copyright law.

YOU CAN BE AN ACTOR, TOO,

If you know just what to do.

IS PERFORMING for
the crowd YOUR THING?

CAN YOU DANCE?

CAN YOU SING?

COSTUME CHANGES curtain calls,
yellow lights AND MONOLOGUES.

IF ALL THESE THINGS SOUND GOOD TO YOU,

then acting for
the stage might do.

Is the CAMERA
MORE YOUR SPEED?

CLAPPERBOARD

assistant directo

CLAPPERBOARDS and FIRST A.D.'s

Honey wagons, blocking spots,

LEARNING LINES FOR ONE TAKE SHOTS.
DIRECTORS SHOUTING BACK TO ONE,

MOVIE ACTING'S LOTS OF FUN.

IF ACTING'S WHAT YOU WANT TO DO,
There will be days you'll have to choose.

Will you miss a birthday bash,
TO PRACTICE FOR A FILM CALLBACK?

FUN AND GAMES WILL HAVE TO WAIT,

THERE ARE LINES TO LEARN,
and two more takes.

If acting is YOUR FAVORITE THING, YOU'LL CHOOSE IT OVER ANYTHING.

THE NEXT THING THAT WE HAVE TO DO, IS FIGURE OUT WHAT TYPE ARE YOU?

Are you short? Are you tall?

Do you have a southern drawl?

Do you have a HERO'S HEART?
Or are you SUPER DUPER SMART?

ACTING COSTS
1. HEAD SHOTS
2. RESUME

ONCE YOU KNOW THE TYPES YOU ARE, IT'S EASY TO SUBMIT FOR PARTS.

TWO HEADSHOTS AND A RESUME, WILL GET YOU STARTED RIGHT AWAY.

CYNDY JONES

KATIE SMITH

The first headshot
is very natural,
And just being you,
is satisfactual.

The second one is much more fun,
Smile for the camera 3 — 2- 1!

YOUR RESUME'S YOUR FINAL TASK,
What's that? What's that?
I'M GLAD YOU ASKED.

Actor's Full Name
Non - Union

Hair:
Height: Eyes:
Weight:

Theater: Role   School/Theater
Play/Production

Training: Acting   Length of Time
Theater School   Voice   Lenght of Time
Singing Coach   Instrument   Lenght of Time
Music Coach

Skills: Horseback riding, roller skating and tennis.

A resume's purpose
is to show who you are.
It tells what you do
and your training thus far.

FIND ACTING PARTS
CLOSE TO HOME,
IN FILMS AND PLAYS
BEFORE YOU ROAM.

A regional agent is what you need
YOU HAVE TO HAVE ONE TO SUCCEED.

10% of what you make for union jobs is what they take.

Non-union work is a little more 20% is what they score.

You've got an audition, that's totally great!
You'll soon go to casting for your big break!

Try not to wear LOGOS, DRESS
IN CLOTHES THAT YOU LIKE.
IF YOU WANT TO STAND OUT,
wear clothes that are bright!

Try not to
wear black,
white or red if you can,
You want to look like YOU
and avoid being GLAM.

Be sure you're on time and make sure you're prepared,
HAVE LOTS OF FUN, NO NEED TO BE SCARED.

But if you are nervous and things get too tough,
JUST BE YOURSELF 'cause being YOU is enough.

Now I've shared ALL MY SECRETS,
THERE'S NO MORE TO TELL.
I WISH YOU GOOD LUCK,
and I wish you well.

AND YOU CAN BE AN ACTOR TOO,
cause now you know just what to do.

ACTOR

Made in the USA
Middletown, DE
08 February 2021

33306460R10015